Polishing the DIAMOND in the ROUGH!

Success is Natural

Five stages to success and the seven elements that define it

Mason Weaver

Motivated Publishing Ventures

ISBN: 987-0-9784415-3-1
Printed in Canada

First Edition: December 2007

Acknowledgements

First and foremost, I acknowledge and thank God, who inspires and empowers me to succeed. Without His wisdom, this book could not have been written.

To Brynda, my wife, thank you for all of the encouragement and support that you so unselfishly lavish upon me.

Thank you to all of the leaders in my life — your advice and prayers have certainly helped me to get to where I am today.

And a special thanks to I.C. Jackson, who's editing skills and hard work helped to bring it all together.

May God bless all of you,

Mason Weaver

Acknowledgments

First and foremost, I acknowledge and thank God, who inspires and empowers me to succeed. Without His wisdom, this book could not have been written.

To Iesha, my wife, thank you for all of the encouragement and support that you have unfailingly given me.

Thank you to all of the leaders in my life — your advice and experience were crucial in helping me to get to where I am today.

And a special thank you to D.C. Jackson, whose editing skills and hard work helped to bring it all together.

May God bless all of you.

Mason Weaver

Foreword

Success in business, as in all things, starts and ends with the way you think. The opinion you have of yourself and your capabilities, the way you view the problem that you are trying to solve — it all boils down to what and how you think. You can never be more competent or successful than you think you can. Your possibilities and your limitations are defined by your mind. So, as we take this journey toward success together, understand that what you are really doing is learning how to think. Put everything that you have previously believed aside and let us start fresh...

Question: Which is more damaging, to think that no one is smarter than you or to think that everyone is smarter than you?

You may not understand what this question has to do with business, but it actually has everything to do with it. Throughout my experience

conducting debates and seminars, delivering sermons and lectures, I have come across both types of people, and not just in the audiences. From noted experts to elected officials, all tend to conduct their business based upon their feelings in the face of facts. Most people fall into one of the two categories, thinking that they are smarter than everyone else or that everyone else is smarter than them.

The "No-one-is-smarter-than-me" crowd will depend upon their college degrees or position within society to validate them. If they have titles behind their names they think it gives legitimacy to all that they would think or say. Any idiot can get a PhD from a committee of idiots...

Then you have the "Everyone-is-smarter-than-me" crowd. They will sit in the audience and judge a debate based on which speaker has the best delivery. These are the people who will argue a point because they read it somewhere. They tend to take things at face value, not yet knowing how to read between the lines, not discerning that those who think they are smarter than everyone else really aren't all that smart...

Have you found yourself in one of these two groups?

The good news is that there is a third group, of which I am a member; the "Follow-the-facts-not-the-feelings" crowd. The "facts" as you see them may or may not be correct, but they will give you a foundation to stand upon. Following the facts has led to my faith, business endeavors, political affiliations, and friendships. The honest pursuit of facts will give your opinions the companion of confidence. When you have to make decisions, you can make them without fear when you know the facts. When you are challenged, it will not matter which questions come up or what the opinions of others will be if yours are based on facts instead of feelings.

For example, here are some popular issues that have come up in recent national debates and the facts that surround them:

The divorce rate in America is 50%. FACT: The rate is under 5% and has never been over 10%. Source: (US Census Bureau)

The Unemployment rate is very high. FACT: The rate is 4.6%, near the all time low. Source: (Department of Labor Statistics)

The rich pay no income taxes. FACT: The top 5% wage earners pay over 50% of income taxes. Source: (IRS)

This is the worst economy in 50 years. FACT: Income is high, the stock market is high, and consumer confidence is high. Source: (Department of Labor Statistics)

I'd bet these facts come as a complete surprise to you. Feel free to check them; remember, I follow the facts, not my feelings or the feelings of others. Some people base their opinions upon what they have heard, which is usually from only one source, and those types of people tend to choose the wrong people to listen to. For example, only one place collects data on deaths, marriages, divorces, and many other statistics. So, we can debate the divorce rate all day long, but the government is the only place where the data is collected. As you gasped in surprise at the facts I listed and compared them to the "facts" that you have read or heard, did you think about where you got your "facts"? I would bet any amount of money that you did not get them from the only reliable source for such statistics; government records.

Only the government issues divorce decrees, so they are the only resource for the divorce records. If one person claims the rate is 50% and I claim it has never been over 10%, a truth seeker should be able to determine the truth from the feeling. It should not matter whether or not I speak more eloquently than the other person or whether I have more supporters in the room. Seek the truth, it will set you free.

Logic tells us that information is valuable. Facts, when learned and properly used, are important indicators of direction and decisions. Why are we so frightened by facts? We may be afraid of what the facts will tell us about our beliefs and the people we have trusted. As we grow and mature, our trusted sources for information shift. We no longer believe in the Tooth Fairy or the Easter Bunny; however, it does not mean that we were foolish when we did believe. It simply means that we have matured; we now have better discernment, and can make better choices. This is

how we should look at our position in life. Right now, take a long, hard, discerning look at your socioeconomic status. If you cannot justify the income level at which you are living, then justify the change of lifestyle that will create better choices for you. Take a look at the facts of your life, and make a decision...

Following the facts causes you to learn and believe the truth. Following the facts will also inspire others to follow you.

Are your opinions based upon the truth or feelings? Do you run your business based on how you feel or what you know? If you realize that you have been running your life and your business on feelings alone, then you are about to be set free. This book will help you to change your way of thinking, and that will help you to change your way of life. You are a *Diamond in the Rough*; it's time to smooth out the rough edges and come forth, truly becoming as valuable as you know you can be.

Table of Contents

Chapter

1

Stages of Success

Most of you who are reading this book are doing so because you believed that some secret to success would be revealed. You suspected that you will be able to plug this 'secret' into your current routine, and if you just follow the directions, you will become successful. I hate to disappoint you, but there is no golden egg. The real secret is that there is no secret; success is natural. As nature takes its course, the end result of that natural progression is success.

The real secret is that there is no secret; success is natural.

This truth may cause you some understandable frustration; you might ask, 'if success is so natural, why haven't I achieved it yet? Where is my natural success?' The longer that you have been in business with only little to moderate success, the more you will reject this truth until you understand the basics of this chapter. It is much easier to follow your feelings than it is to follow the facts, and you might feel like success couldn't possibly be natural because you haven't stumbled upon it yet. However, after completing this chapter, you will come to realize that success, and yes, your success in particular, is natural, and that you are more capable of achieving it than you knew. If you learn to allow nature to produce success, your efforts will contribute only to your future successes and not the mediocrity that you may be used to.

And that's a fact...

If you learn to allow nature to produce success, your efforts will contribute only to your future successes and not the mediocrity that you may be used to.

Are You Working Against Nature?

Adulthood (as we know it, anyway) is a mental illness. Our society, our peers, and our own insecurities have taught us what we can and cannot do. We have learned to define ourselves by our failures instead of our drive and aspirations. So, now we can't think straight. We sabotage our own efforts, convincing ourselves of shortcomings that don't exist, learning to live under the thumb of others, teaching our children to do the same. When someone's thinking and actions cause detriment to themselves they are said to be mentally ill. However, this behavior is what we have learned to call 'being a responsible adult.'

We sabotage our own efforts, convincing ourselves of shortcomings that don't exist...

In order to think this way, you actually have to work against nature. Consider the mind of a child; he does not think about failure when he sets out to do something. The child only thinks about the end result of his efforts — his success. He may try over and over again before getting it right, but he continues to try because he doesn't know what else to do. He doesn't yet know how to give up and hang his head in shame. He has to learn that from older people who were taught to do the same by others. For something he wants badly enough, he understands only the pursuit of it, using failures as learning tools and stepping stones toward the eventual acquisition of what he desires. The way a child pursues a goal is considered naïve by the mentally ill, but it is actually the force of an animal-like instinct that is absolutely natural. Needless to say, children get what they want much more often than adults do.

Don't think about failure when you set out to do something.

So who's really naïve?

Babies Become Teachers

Success is natural and reachable. We all have the desire to achieve whatever we can dream. If success is natural and reachable, then why are we falling short of achieving it? Maybe we either lose the nature or lose the reach. However, something must happen to the human psyche to remove the eagerness to reach the next level.

Think about the lessons a little baby could teach us. Even before the child is born it is seeking freedom. The mother keeps the baby warm, comfortable, fed, and loved. The child has everything it could ever want right there in the mother's womb. The child has never been told it will be free of mother one day. No one tells the child how nice it is to be free of mother. The child has only known the comfort and love of mother's womb. Yet one day it will struggle to be free of her. In spite of all the love and attention the mother gives her child, the baby will still seek the unknown avenue of freedom. Why? Because freedom is natural.

Freedom is natural!

Once the mother gives birth, she will bring the child home and do nothing but love the child. Mother will keep the child fed, burped, changed, bathed, and warm. Even the slightest whimper will have mother up at the child's side, ready to provide for every need. The mother will hold the child lovingly in her arms and rock the child to sleep. But, still, after months of love, affection, and attention, the child will struggle out of mother's arms onto the floor to start crawling. Why? Because freedom is natural.

The freedom that babies seek leads to success in their endeavors. From walking to running to driving the family car, they continue to grow and develop in this way until adulthood. It is the natural cycle of life. To a healthy human being in his most natural state, the desire for freedom will eventually bring about progress, which inevitably

leads to success. It is the unhealthy and the unnatural that causes us to fail. Our unhealthy and unnatural attitudes are what keep us from wholeheartedly seeking the freedom that we are supposed to experience. What do you want to be free from? Employment? Debt? Dependency?

Our attitudes are what keep us from seeking the freedom we are supposed to experience.

Allow your thirst for freedom to awaken the natural instinct inside of you.

The Laws of Nature

Nature itself is a set of life cycles and their respective laws. Natural things are things that grow and develop by a set of unchanging standards; the laws of nature. The reason that you have yet to experience the success you are striving for is that you don't know the natural laws of success. If you did, you would follow them. Since you don't know them, you are almost absolutely breaking them.

There are three basic laws of nature as they relate to success:

1. Success is the natural result of progress, and progress takes place in stages.

2. Nature does not allow you to pass from one stage of development to the next until you have mastered the stage you are in.

3. You will become a product of your social and intellectual environments.

If you attempt to defy these laws, you will become counterproductive and remain unsuccessful. The law of gravity dictates that you can't jump out of a tree and float safely to the

ground. Likewise, the natural laws of success cannot be ignored without consequence.

Have you tried to become successful while constantly looking behind you? Are you always focused on the past or trying to drag baggage and people with you to your future? If so, you are regressing and not progressing. You should be looking and moving forward, not backward. Once a baby comes through the birth canal, it never tries to go back. Although a baby's adaptation to his new environment takes time, he simply grows little by little, leaving the old things behind and moving on to the new. If you are still holding on to old, ineffective beliefs, practices, and people, you are breaking the first law.

You should be looking and moving forward, not backward

Did you get into business because you were really excited about the product and opportunity presented to you only to be disappointed because, despite your best efforts, the success the heavy hitters promised seems to be out of your reach even though you did exactly what they told you to do? If so, you probably are trying to defy the second law. The top producers in your company or industry did not get there overnight, and neither will you. If you have not mastered the first stages of success, how do you expect to waltz on down to the finish line? You can't give a toddler the keys to your car and expect him to drive; he can't just instantaneously become mature and coherent enough to operate a motor vehicle. He has to grow into maturity in order to be successful, and so do you.

What are you eating? Where are you living? Who are you surrounded by? Those factors determine your health, outlook, and quality of life. The people and information that you expose yourself to have the same effect on your psyche and your actions. Are you still spending your time socializing with people who have little to no drive, talent, influence, or integrity? Are you still wasting time absorbing negative and nonessential

information from your media sources and companions? You will never become successful by feeding yourself things that only encourage or support failure. Don't think that your environment supports failure? If it does not specifically promote and produce progress, it supports failure; period. There is no gray area or middle ground; it is a law of nature. If you expose yourself to the elements for long enough, you will become ill. Keep yourself warm, fed, and exercised, and you will gain strength. If you do what you've always done and stay where you've always been, you will get what you've always gotten, guaranteed.

The people and information that you expose yourself to have the same effect on your psyche and your actions.

So, if you are ready to grow up and progress your way to success, you will have to familiarize yourself with the stages of success. Once you know where you are, you can determine what you need to do to get where you want to go.

Don't waste time absorbing negative and nonessential information from your media sources and companions

The Stages of Success

This book will expound upon some of the essential habits and characteristics necessary for success with respect to the stage in which they are developed or cultivated. That way, you not only learn what you need to do, but you also learn when you can expect to really blossom in each particular area. Although a person begins to speak as a young toddler, it is not until adolescence that he begins to

master the language that he has been taught. In the same way, you will already possess certain qualities, but as you grow into the appropriate stages, you will then begin to see them take precedence in your business endeavors.

Stage One
- A Baby Walks: Gaining Self Confidence

The baby who is developmentally ready to walk continues to crawl until he decides to try walking. Understand that you do not teach a child to walk. The child must first have the desire and determination to walk. Until then, there is nothing you can do. The child has to master crawling first.

Then, one day, the child will pull himself up on the edge of the coffee table. The child is not trying to get something off of the table; he has a new mission. The child has observed that if walking could be mastered, he could get the candy or bottle without having to get your attention. The child knows that walking is a key to freedom from dependency upon you.

The parent watches the child hold on to the edge of the coffee table and nervously let go. The child's mind, however, is not yet on walking; it is on falling. So what does the child do? Fall. That is where the mind is. You will head towards what you think, so the child's behind heads towards the floor.

You will head towards what you think...

But this failure does not stop the child. As a matter of fact, doctors say a child will fall about three hundred times before taking his first step. Three hundred times in failure before success? How many of us could learn to walk today if we had to fail three hundred times first?

The baby walks when he gains confidence. To begin a business venture without confidence is like

expecting a baby to walk before it believes it can. You will find yourself holding onto the table to catch yourself, "just in case". You must enter a business venture in which you feel confident that you will grow and thrive.

Confidence is key, feel confident that you will grow and thrive!

It does not matter which business you go into. People have made millions in every business under the sun. It is not the type of business that makes one successful, it is the approach. There is not one oddball business venture in which someone has not made millions. From barbershops to the Pet Rock, recycling cans to Post It® sticky notes, someone has made millions doing it. On the other hand, you can get a MBA, a law degree, or even graduate from the best medical school in the nation and still go broke. For instance, it has been documented that most people with law degrees do not work in the legal field. Yet, we all know of the high priced, high profile lawyers that the entertainment media glorifies so often. It is not their education, intelligence, or type of practice pursued that makes those lawyers successful as opposed to all the others who passed the Bar Exam. It is the confidence of those individuals coupled with their maturity that sets them apart.

Are you confident that the business you are in can sustain you? Are you still like the baby who is holding onto the edge of the table, sure that you will fall if you let go? While it may be unwise to quit your day job as soon as you open your doors, you must have the confidence that you will soon be in business full time and will no longer need to work for someone else. After all, isn't that the point?

Do you know what the point of your business is? What do you want?

Stage Two
- On the Playground:
Picking the Right Team

One of the most important things a young child does is pick his friends. As a toddler, he would play with anyone who was willing and available. However, as the young child becomes a more coherent individual, he becomes more selective concerning who he spends his playtime with. Confident children enjoy the luxury of choosing for themselves who they will associate with. Shy and insecure children usually just fall in with whoever will accept them. Those confident children become leaders as they grow and mature. Those who are successful in business are leaders, and good leaders know how to choose the right support team.

Good leaders know how to choose the right support team.

The type of personality you have may determine how you view your team. You may consider them to be like a family, an army, or even like a sports team. No matter how you conceptualize your support team, you must know how to surround yourself with the people who will help propel you to your next level and only those people. Everyone else, no matter how much you love them, will hinder you.

Surround yourself with only the people who will help propel you to your next level.

So how do you know who to choose? You will know exactly who you need to seek as you begin to discern who to let go. Most of us never get to truly move forward with the right people because we are still associating with the wrong people. The influence of the wrong people will absolutely, positively, always poison your thinking and stop

progress right in its tracks. (Remember the laws of nature?)

Who to let go of is simple: anyone who does not directly support your endeavors is out. Whether for morale or special skills, your circle needs to be full of those who can offer some type of support. Doubters simply have no positive effect on your efforts, which means they serve no purpose. Whether these doubters are family members, lifelong friends, or even ill-matched business partners, anyone who isn't ready to run needs to be benched. They don't have to become enemies; you can still see them at holiday dinners and other special functions. However, they no longer get to take up time in your day-to-day life because from now on, you are focused on building your business. So why waste time with anyone who would tear it down?

Doubters simply have no positive effect on your efforts, which means they serve no purpose.

Letting go and leaving where you are is very difficult. Your heartstrings may be stretched to their limits, and at first you may even feel remorse. Don't; this isn't personal; it's business. If you don't have the guts to let go of those who would hinder you at this early stage in your business life, how will you be able to face the challenges to come? If you have the confidence in yourself and your business, then you have to have the strength to move on without those who have been living in your comfort zone. If you don't have it already, this is the stage in which you will begin to develop the instinct to let go of anyone and anything that doesn't support progress.

Letting go and leaving where you are is very difficult; it's not personal; it's business.

In order to let go of the dead weight, you absolutely must begin to surround yourself with

those who can help you. No man is an island; you're not going to be able to do this all by yourself. It's now time to be outgoing and ambitious; time to meet new people and strengthen relationships with acquaintances who can become assets. As you develop the positive relationships, the ones that are negative will become less and less important to you. Then you can clearly focus on how to leverage the talents and people available to you.

Focus on how to leverage the talents and people available to you

If you were in charge of choosing a basketball team, would you choose all tall people? Of course not; you need the short person to handle the ball, the mid-sized person to drive to the basket, and the tall center to block shots and hit the boards. You will need a mixture of individuals, all bringing their skills into play.

However, everyone who seems like a good fit will not (and oftentimes should not) make the team. It would be very difficult to build a basketball team from people who do not like playing basketball. If you had a strong enough personality or charisma, you probably could convince five otherwise uninterested people to join your team, but at what cost? Sure, you could be such a great coach that you may inspire five apathetic people to really play their hearts out and win the championship. But that is for Hollywood movies, not reality.

Reality would dictate you choose your five players from those already interested in the game and who have a passion for it. They would be eager to join you and would have enough motivation to learn from you. Your team cannot include your best friend or cousin if they have no interest. Likewise, your team may include someone you have never worked with but, because of their skills and motivation, would be a true asset.

This is the winning approach to all team building. Build the team with people that already have the goals of the team. If it is a business team, make sure they all love the business goals and direction.

Build your team with people who already have the goals of the team or that love the goals and direction of the team.

But what if you don't know anyone like that? How do you build a team with no players?

That is why you network; commit to meeting two new people a day. Whether in person or online, put yourself in a position to meet as many new people as possible, no matter what field they are in. All of your connections won't become team members or customers, but if you are diligent, you will find those who will best compliment you and your efforts along the way. You will recognize team members when you see them because you will be mutually beneficial to each other. You may not offer each other the same level of benefit, but you will be able to link efforts and move forward together.

Pick people who think like you, share the same goals, and have the same level of confidence.

Network; commit to meeting two new people a day. You will find those who will best compliment you and your efforts.

Stage Three
- Adolescence: The Awkward Stage

Once you have learned to stand on your own two feet and have established your team, it is now time to move forward. Just like learning to drive a car or riding a bike for the first time, you will find your forward movement a little hard to guide. This is the first real test. The obstacles will seem large, and for the most part, your personal experience has not been extensive enough to give you a lot of wisdom on how to handle it all. Most of your life you have been either an employee or a student, most of your friends have never owned a business, you have not developed enough business associates yet, and your own expertise in business has not given you enough insight to anticipate the next steps. This is a very vulnerable stage of development.

This is why it is important to surround yourself with people going in the same direction you are going. When the storms break out and things look the darkest, it may not be only the wise words of a leader that brings you back on course. They have already made it; their wisdom and experience is valuable. Others on the same level as you, going through it at the same time may speak to you about the dream you shared with them. It will be your message of confidence given back to you that will also get you over the rough parts. Gain your strength in advance by surrounding yourself with people who believe in your dream.

Surround yourself with people who believe in your dream.

If you only have your old friends as allies and they do not support your dream, guess what? They will encourage you to stop your foolishness and return to the things you have always done with them. They are not going anywhere and they do not want you to, either. It is not because they do not like you; they love you...just where you are.

If you sit around every night with your old friends doing the things you have become

comfortable doing, any change becomes a threat to the comfort level. If you have five buddies sitting around the house complaining about being broke, how there are no pay raises, and how tired they are of depending upon the company to give them more benefits, the circular conversation could go on forever. But if you decide not to spend your nights sitting around with them complaining, but instead decided to spend that time developing an escape plan, the entire group might come against you. What else can they do? After years of complaining about the corporate big whigs, business owners, and goal oriented people, they survive it all only to see one of their own striving to be one? This will never end positively.

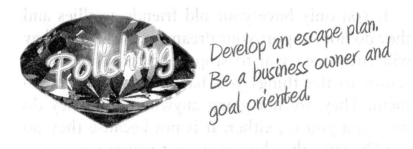

Develop an escape plan. Be a business owner and goal oriented.

This is why when workers become managers they stop hanging around workers and begin hanging around other managers. It's not because they think they are better than the workers, but they are certainly different. Now that you are different, you must emerge from your former environment. However, doing so will prove to be a process that does not go smoothly at all. This is the stage in which you absolutely let go of all the dead weight, because you are preparing to accelerate, and only those who are ready to run can come with you.

Emerge from your former environment, let go of the dead weight and prepare to accelerate!

Just like the adolescent who struggles to find himself and express himself adequately, you will face challenges that you may not always handle perfectly. However, if you have the confidence and the right support, you will make it through. Like an adolescent, you will make it because you are

thoroughly convinced that you are right and that you are capable. You have the right mindset and the right support, and you know that you are on the right track.

Although adolescents make mistakes, their best quality is actually their inflated sense of self-worth. If you don't truly believe that you are right in what you are doing, the pressure at this stage could put you out of business for good. Instead of discouraging you, the objections of those who cannot go where you are going should actually remind you of why you are in business in the first place, making your resolve to go forward even stronger.

This is how nature operates. It actually takes a bit of an ego for you to go into business for yourself. Just think about it; you are saying you can make a widget better than someone else can. To some that is prideful, and maybe even condescending. But, how can you go into business thinking you will only be as good as others? You must take the stance of excellence before you begin this venture. I do not see any difference in politicians, actors, basketball players, home builders, or auto mechanics; they all go into their respective endeavors striving to be the very best. That is a closed, narrow minded, egotistical point of view; it is also the correct point of view for success in business.

Take the stance of excellence!

Please read carefully; I know I am going to lose some of you right here. I am not saying that you should think that you are better than anyone else, but you cannot think that anyone is more capable than you. There is a difference between being better at something and being more capable than someone else. A young athlete on a team could play with a more skilled player on the same team and still have the capability to become even better than him. You must have confidence in your

capability before you can take advantage of your skills.

Tiger Woods possessed the capability of becoming the world's most dominate golfer even as a child, but he could not become the best golfer until he turned his capabilities into abilities. At ten years old, Tiger Woods had the capability to become the winner of the US Open, but he did not yet have the skills to do it. He had to hang around other golfers, play the game, develop knowledge, and exercise his skills for years. He could not play softball with the guys, hang out at the bar with his high school buddies, or only show up on game day without practice. Tiger became Tiger by going after it like a tiger.

Stage Four
- The Teenagers: Sprouting Toward Success

This is when all of the preparation of the first three stages begins to pay off. Think of the teenagers and young adults you have encountered in your life that have shown great potential. It is during these years that they really begin to shine.

Although they are not fully mature and they certainly aren't perfect, they begin to distinguish themselves from others and garner the attention of those who are mature and can see the unlimited possibilities within them. These young adults begin to walk into a realm of possibility and opportunity that they have never known, and it can get intense. Scholarships are offered, internships are acquired, and mentors arrive, willing to help guide them toward their futures. Future success is now guaranteed if one can just stay the course and take advantage of all the opportunities presented.

This stage is when you begin to really produce in your business; you are finally making some real money, and those at the top begin to take you seriously. While you have already received significant help from your leaders in order to get where you are now, others who have not been directly involved in your development will begin to take notice. The ripple effect causes growth spurts, and like a sprouting plant, you and your business seem to grow in great strides and not gradually as you had been. At this stage, if you can just perform the balancing act necessary to handle it all, you will begin to fall into the groove of the fast track that

you are on, and success will soon no longer be a goal, but a lifestyle for you.

Stage Five
- Maturity: Managing Success

You're all grown up, and now you are living the dream. It is in this stage that you remain, growing as you learn to manage your success. You begin to focus on leveraging the future of your business because you have already built it. You focus on retirement instead of monthly income now. This is also the time when you begin to help others who are sprouting come up to where you are. There is less work, more play, and now, instead of you working for the money, the money is working for you. Few people make it this far; but it's not because they didn't have the capability to make it. Those who do not master the previous stages are simply not allowed access to this lifestyle.

Will you be one of the few? Are you really a diamond in the rough? If so, it is time to be refined. Dare to acquire the elements necessary to shape and polish your future. Become the jewel you envision in your dreams...

Polish your future. Focus on leveraging the future and get your money working for you

If you are ready, let us start from the very beginning...

Element 1:
Desire

Mastering the first stage of success requires that you gain self confidence, but it starts with the desire to be free. The desire to be free is what inspires you to begin the journey toward progress. Although we have to endure the bumps and bruises of learning through trial and error, search and discovery, the entire process begins with the first sparks of desire. Do you truly desire to be free from your current circumstances? Surely you assume that the answer to that question is, "Yes." However, if you aren't tired of being where you are, you don't yet have the desire I speak of.

The desire to be free is what inspires you to begin the journey toward progress.

Remember the baby; he will only walk when he is tired of crawling and watching others walk without him. Until it pains you to see others walking, you really won't have what it takes to get up and walk for yourself. Why? Because learning to walk costs you something. There is pain in the falling. There is frustration in the constant rejection. You have to have the will to continue to strive even when others are passing you by. If you are not really tired of being on the outside looking in, you won't be able to muster the willpower to do what it takes to succeed. The baby who desires to walk gains confidence each time he makes a significant stride toward walking, but his desire is what really keeps him going.

Learning will cost you something...

Are You Tired Yet?

Understand that there is a difference between being tired of one's own circumstances and being

jealous of someone else's success. Jealousy likes to masquerade as desire, but it is an imposter. Jealousy of someone who is successful may cause you to ask yourself, "If he can do it, why can't I?" However, it won't get you too far past the starting line. Many people get into business for themselves because they don't believe that "the rich" should have all the resources, and that they deserve to have control over their own lives, too. The problem with that kind of thinking is that your success is not a competition with anyone else, just like your failure to succeed is not anyone else's fault. You going into business for yourself should have little to do with the accomplishments of others and more to do with your own desires for yourself and your family. "The rich" are who they are because they once had a desire to change their circumstances. They didn't get to where they are by trying to "stick it to 'the man'." You won't make it that way, either.

Going into business for yourself should have little to do with the accomplishments of others and more to do with your own desires for yourself and your family.

There is, however, a healthy role that 'the powers that be' play in your desire to be free. They should inspire you to be more like them and less like those who depend on them. It is the dependency, not the people themselves that should make you sick and tired. You should be tired of having to depend on others for your livelihood, not tired of them succeeding and you being left behind. Can you see the difference in the two mentalities?

There is no crime in being hugely successful; after all, isn't that what you want? Don't you want your business to grow to such a point where you have more employees than you can manage yourself? More locations? More product lines? Don't you want to be at the top of a growing organization? While everyone's desires may not be to be rich and famous, anyone who wants to go into business should have a healthy desire for a business that can constantly and consistently grow. That is the only way that you will have something to leave to your children or those for whom you want to build a future. Costs and taxes always go up, so if your business doesn't grow, the needs of those you leave it to will soon outgrow it. Therefore, your desire should be for a business that

will continue to grow, and if you don't have that kind of desire, you probably won't have any kind of business for very long.

How Badly Do You Want It?

Have you ever seen a lazy baby? Some babies don't walk until after their first birthday. While such delayed development is no cause for alarm for a parent, it is a sign that the baby's desire to walk was not as strong as it could have been. Most babies walk before they are a year old, and the baby who doesn't usually enjoys the attention he gets from having to be carried more than he desires to be free. In your first stage toward success, this can be a harmful characteristic if it is one that you possess. You have to want to be free badly enough to let go of all of the 'perks' of dependency.

Do you still want someone to carry you? Do you still think that the world owes you something? Are you still looking for the easy way out or to get rich quick? If so, you are like the baby who still wants someone to carry them. If you really want

freedom badly enough, you will do whatever you have to do to stand on your own two feet and walk. Sometimes it means that you may have to walk alone. It always means that there will be significant sacrifices. However, for the person who really wants to succeed, the necessary sacrifices are well worth the blood, sweat, and tears. The freedom that you seek has to be worth the journey.

Sometimes it means that you have to walk alone.

Dreams into Goals

Most of us have dreams that we hope will become reality one day. We start as children, pondering the possibilities of life and thinking about all the things we want but do not yet have.

As we grow older, some of us allow life to drain us, robbing us of our dreams. However, many of us manage to keep hope alive, and thus, we dream.

But how do we make our dreams come true?

Most people have absolutely no idea. That's why so many of us have dreams instead of the lives we truly want to live. The missing piece of the puzzle is how to make those dreams real. Fantasies can't put food on the table, clothes on your back, or kids in college. The process of growing up and making a living has been an exhausting one for most of us; so, those who manage to have some drive left tend to focus on achieving their dreams.

Have the drive to focus on achieving your dreams.

Consider this: as few of us as there are that are still chasing our dreams, even fewer are looking to

achieve our goals. Who has the hope and energy to set goals, much less achieve them?

I can tell you who — the people who are living their dreams.

Those of us who are blessed to see the connection between the two end up becoming successful. You don't just wake up one day living your dreams; you turn dreams into goals, and goals into reality. The bridge is not built from dreams to reality; it is built from dreams to goals.

Turn your dreams into goals, and goals into reality.

Here is an example: a young man reads his favorite car magazine, and he fantasizes about the Ferrari in the centerfold. It is a dream of his to own that Ferrari; he meditates on it day and night,

thinking of where he would drive it and how fast he would go. However, the young man only has a couple thousand dollars to spend, so he goes to the local used car lot to see what he can find within his price range. When he finds something that he reasonably likes, he sets out to buy it, and after negotiating with the car salesman, he makes the purchase.

The young man dreamt of a Ferrari, but his goal was to attain affordable transportation. While he achieved that goal, the dream still went unrealized. Why? Because he didn't think that he could achieve his dream. He knew that a Ferrari would cost much more than what he had, but he was confident that he could get a used car with the resources he had on hand. He set a reasonable goal, and attained it, leaving the dream on his pillow.

The difference between a dream and a goal is that a dream is something that you think would be nice if it ever came true and a goal is something that you expect to achieve. What successful people do is, instead of setting reasonable goals like the young man in the example and most other "responsible adults", they set goals based on their dreams. They actually convert dreams into goals.

A goal is something that you expect to achieve.

'How do they do that,' you ask?

Through a little known modern invention called planning. You turn dreams into goals by creating a plan.

Turn dreams into goals by creating a plan.

Do you have what it takes to turn a Dream into a Goal?

There is a surefire way to find out. If you have the work ethic of a successful businessperson, you

can achieve your dreams. But it all starts with the sacrifices. Try this for 30 days:

Turn off the television; unplug it, take off the cord and mail it to yourself. Get it out of your life.

Create a routine for the extra time and follow it religiously.

☑ Read

☑ Make business calls

☑ Study your product

☑ Build your team

☑ Make a commitment to your team and make it measurable for everyone

☑ Read one book a month

☑ Listen to one audio a day

☑ Meet two new people a day

If you do this, you will graduate to a new level of productivity. You will at least know that if the solution works then the problem is you. If you can do it for 30 days, you can do it for 30 months. Most successful income producing plans only require around 30-36 months to create. You have to decide if it will be 30 months at a time or one month AND 6 months off.

If you can do something for 30 days, you can do it for 30 months.

Don't get discouraged if you can't keep the commitment for the whole 30 days the first time that you try. You may not be able to do it for 30 days, just like someone who goes to the gym for the first time in 30 years. It can be a bit overwhelming. However, do not decide that you can't do it until you try it for 3 days.

If you can do it for 3 days, you can do it for 30 days.

If you can do it for 30 days, you can do it for 30 months.

This kind of work ethic may take some trial and error to develop, but your desire for success that burns within you will give you the energy you need to make it happen. You can do this if you really want to.

Your desire for success that burns within you will give you the energy you need to make it happen.

Remember, it is your desire that starts the fire...

Chapter 3

Element 2: Vision

Most people don't consider themselves to be visionaries; that title is usually reserved for great people who go on to achieve great things. However, in order to be successful in business, you not only have to see yourself as one of those special people; you actually have to be one. Actually, this isn't as difficult or even as special as it sounds. A visionary is just someone who has a vision, and vision is simply seeing clearly the problem as well as the solution.

Vision is simply seeing the problem and the solution clearly.

If you think about it, that's what a business owner is.

Products and services exist to serve needs. So, if you are having a hard time moving your inventory, you may not have yet identified the persons who have the want or need that it fulfills. This is, in business, what is called 'finding your target market.' Many business owners, particularly those small and home business owners who produce their own goods and may not have conducted extensive market research, may be promoting a product or service that does not fulfill a common want or need or may not fulfill wants and needs as effectively or efficiently as possible. In either circumstance, there is a need for vision before there will be success.

Know your target market.

In order to have a useful product or service, you must solve a problem. If there is no want or need that your product or service fulfills, you won't sell much, if any, of what you are offering. That makes

sense, right? If you can solve the problem, that means you have already identified it and have the remedy as well. As people learn about the remedy, they will begin to do business with the problem solver. So, a successful business owner is, by definition, a visionary.

By definition, a successful business owner is a visionary.

See how great you are?

Remember, success is natural, and you are confident that you can achieve it (or you are at least building that confidence in the first stage of success), so, although you may not yet be successful in business, you know that you soon will be. However, the primary obstacle that stands between your vision and its realization is a big word called "leadership."

The primary obstacle that stands between you and your vision, is leadership.

Consider the religious leader...

When someone is called to the ministry of God, they may start a church. Well, the church vision is only known to the pastor. The vision is not given to each member of the church, only to the pastor. The pastor must show leadership qualities in order for the congregation to follow him. As he goes

through the building plan, expansion of the ministries, and church organization, his leadership will be essential. Others will have different ideas on what the direction of the church should be. However, the vision of the pastor cannot be altered because he is easily swayed by others. Many will leave because they did not see the vision. But the church pastor has to stay focused on his vision, and if he does, he will one day stand in the sanctuary of his vision.

The visionary must be able to lead those who have the tools to make the vision a reality.

In order for a vision to come to pass, the visionary must be able to lead those who have the necessary tools to make the vision a reality. Even if your business is a sole proprietorship, you have to deal with other people in order to achieve your business objectives. Most businesses move forward through the work of teams and require extensive team building, which we will discuss in detail in the next chapter. However, whether your team is in-house or a conglomerate of those whom you deal with in order to run your business, only a leader will succeed in getting the job done. If people are going to do what you want and need them to so that you can further your own objectives, you will have to lead them there. Remember, these people have their own needs and wants that they are focused on, so the visionary must find a way to convince those whom he works with to actually work.

Can you handle that?

Many of you are probably saying, "No, I can't" to yourselves right now because you have yet to see yourselves as leaders. However, you are; you just have to be so convinced of your vision that you naturally seek to find and motivate those who are ready to bring the vision to pass.

"And just who are those people?" you ask.

Those who are ready to make your vision come to pass are those who can appreciate your

enthusiasm concerning the problem and your courage in working toward the solution. Those who are ready to bring the vision to pass don't have to be primed and pumped; you don't have to beg them to join you or convince them that the problem really is a problem. It's usually easy to identify the problem; what makes you a diamond in the rough is that you have the vision to see the problem and the solution. People who are ready will flock to you.

A good leader knows how to listen to others without being deterred from the vision.

However, know that your being a visionary will not only attract positive people who can contribute to your success, but you will also attract negative people who will try and bring you down. A good leader knows how to listen to others without being deterred from the vision. If you truly have the vision to run a successful business, you can discern what are good suggestions for helping the vision come to pass and what are destructive detours that serve to change your vision into someone else's. Leadership requires absolute conviction concerning the vision and wisdom in dealing with those who will either help or hurt your efforts to produce the solution.

Leadership requires conviction of the vision and wisdom to deal with those who will help or hurt your efforts.

This is true with every aspect of life. Whether it is getting a college degree, raising a family, or building a business, you have to see it completely, the problem and the solution. Then you know the vision is for you.

Chapter

4

Element 3:
Passion

Masonism: If you don't think you can do it, get out of the way of people who can.

If you don't think you can be successful in business, chances are that you won't be. Why? Because it's your expectation that drives you. A baby's desire to walk is not enough to propel him forward. If you don't expect to be successful, your desire for success will only lead to frustration and discouragement because your desire alone doesn't have the power to produce results. While it is true that your desire starts the fire, it is your expectation that fuels the flame. Desire coupled with expectation is what we call 'passion'.

If you don't think you can do it, get out of the way of the people who can.

Notice that I did not say that desire coupled with belief equals passion. You believing that you can do it is not the same as you expecting to do it.

Look at it this way:

Does a pregnant woman believe in a baby or does she expect a baby? Of course, she expects to have the baby, and because of her expectations she buys baby clothes, prepares a nursery, and sees a doctor.

Expectations motivate you to action based upon your vision.

Her expectations motivate her to action based upon her vision. She visualizes her future with her child and begins to prepare for all that she foresees. If she just believed in a baby, she would be inactive. Expecting is a verb. There is no need for

anyone to tell her that one day she will be having a baby; that baby is kicking from the inside trying to get out. She is certain that a baby is coming. Everything in her body is announcing it to her, so she acts accordingly.

When the vision and drive get so deep inside of you that you can feel it moving you, then you expect to win. The feeling has to be powerful enough to drive you forward. It does not matter if it is having a baby or graduating from college, the drive must precede the action; the action is fueled by the expectation. Therefore you can tell the drive of others by the level of expectation in their lives.

Act like you expect to win.

Act like you expect to win.

If you expect to win your leaders will expect you to win also. They will prepare for your arrival to the top. They will guide and direct and establish your training, but you have to expect it enough to show up. If you believe it, act like you believe it; that is expectation.

Expectation is believing and acting like you believe.

This earnest expectation is what propels you into the second stage of success; this is when you start to build your team. Your expectation will cause you to begin gathering your resources, with human resources being the most important. You will begin to get a clear understanding of who needs to be on your team in order for you to bring the vision to pass; what talents and skills are necessary for the task at hand and who has them.

However, developing earnest expectation is harder than it sounds for many entrepreneurs.

When you have failed in the past, your expectation for success in the future naturally goes down. A little discouragement can go a long way. So what do you do when you have failed in business before and find yourself lacking the motivation to honestly expect to win in the present?

Past failures tend to influence your future expectations for success let go of the past.

You forgive yourself.

What does forgiveness have to do with your business? You have to forgive yourself for your previous failure(s). You can't continue to cower in fear at the thought of launching out into the deep because you were disappointed when you tried and did not succeed. You may have been ill-prepared, ignorant, or inefficient, but you are older and wiser now, so you have to release yourself from the bondage of prior mistakes and move on.

Not letting go of past failures kills confidence, and remember, without confidence, a baby can't walk. Before you can move on to the next stage of your success, you first have to master walking. So, walk tall, with confidence, free from the weight of past business blunders.

Don't kill your confidence by hanging on to past failures.

When a confident man has a vision, it produces expectation. When his desire meets that expectation, he becomes passionate.

Chapter

5

Element 4:
Preparation

Benjamin Franklin said, "By failing to prepare, you are preparing to fail", and he couldn't have been more right. Nothing can take the place of proper preparation, and nothing can stop the confident leader who is aptly prepared.

By failing to prepare, you are preparing to fail.

- Benjamin Franklin

Success is natural, and as you acquire the desire, vision, and passion for your business, you will naturally gain momentum in building your team. As you gain passion, you become inspired to talk to people about your business, but it is your preparation that will weed out the wrong people. Your victory in this stage is based on how well you can rally support from the right people, and I can guarantee you that if you are not prepared through education and practice, you will turn the right people off. Successful people like to deal with other successful people, or at least people with great potential. How do you exemplify your potential? By being educated and exercised in general business practice as well as that of your field; you do it by being prepared.

Desire, vision and passion lead to momentum. Preparation will give you the right team.

Although you may be bright, talented, and/or charismatic, if you aren't prepared to properly promote and conduct your business, you will still fail. Oftentimes talented or otherwise gifted people try to "wing it" in business, relying more on personality or aptitude than on good, old-fashioned hard work and preparation. They think that they have an edge, but it can actually be a handicap. People will see you as a hustler instead

of a reputable businessperson, and why wouldn't they? Are you a professional? Do you present yourself in a way that lets people know that you are there to conduct serious business? Do you know basic business terminology and practice? When you contact potential supporters and customers, can they tell that you know what you are talking about?

Be a professional and you'll be taken seriously.

Are you educated on your particular product or service and your industry as a whole? A serious businessperson wants to provide the best product and/or service possible; they are looking to actually solve a problem for the consumer. How can you address my problem if you don't know your product or your market well enough to convince me that you have the solution? Your bright smile isn't going to sell me, but your knowledge of the product line, benefits, and your competition's product will. As a supporter, I want to know that I am dealing with a competent, productive person, not someone playing CEO. My reputation is on the line when I choose to link efforts with you. Yours is too...

Good business is solving a problem for your customer are you prepared?

If "Knowledge is power," what is ignorance? Powerlessness? Studying your vision will not only give you knowledge, but it will also give you the tools to pass on to those you must train. Furthermore, it allows you to create your own record and databases for future problems.

So let's say you are a natural at acquiring information; you know everything there is to know about your product and that of your competition, you've conducted market research, and you are armed with as much information as one brain can hold. Great; but, if you haven't actually tried to sell something, you are only resting on your intellectual laurels, and you are still not truly prepared. **Remember, this is the stage in which you build your team**; you have to have some kind of experience doing what you do to gain the confidence of those with whom you want to work.

"To build a successful team, you must gain their confidence preparation is the key..."

As a young entrepreneur, you may not have as much experience as your competition and contemporaries, but you should have at least practiced the process enough times to have a grasp on what you need to do to succeed. By now, you should be making business calls, networking, selling (or at least attempting to sell) your product or service, and following up with contacts and previous customers. So, when you find a potential benefactor or partner, you can convey your vision with confidence because of experience, which gains their confidence and trust. Otherwise, you are spewing theory and selling dreams, and successful people don't buy into that. Successful people don't do what sounds good, they do what works, and they only build with others who are doing the same.

Successful people don't do what sounds good, they do what works!

Are you prepared?

By the time you reach this second team building, stage of success you should be talking the talk and walking the walk. "Talking the talk" simply means that you are communicating your knowledge, and "walking the walk" is your practicing of the process. The old cliché turns out not to be so 'cliché', huh?

Talking the talk and walking the walk is not a cliché.

Are you talking to people about your business? In order to talk the talk you have to be talking, right? If you aren't talking about your business, then you haven't mastered the fist stage of success development yet; you are lacking in confidence because you lack the proper desire, vision, or passion. Once you have those, you should automatically increase your preparation. In order to be in business, you should quite naturally have business and industry knowledge as well as some experience in conducting business. Now should be the time when you seek out advanced knowledge. You should be talking to people about your vision with passion, and that activity should make you sensitive to the fact that you need to be able to answer any questions or challenges with confidence. People want to follow a leader, particularly one with expert knowledge.

Is that you?

People want to follow a leader who has expert knowledge.

Are you putting yourself out there? Are you marketing your product or service, and are you

networking? If not, you are not prepared to receive business, and your inactivity will take you straight to the poorhouse. Haven't you noticed that your industry and business leaders are always doing something? They are always promoting, marketing, networking, and demonstrating. It's like they are obsessed, right? Have you ever wondered if it really takes all of that? Well, the answer is, yes, it does. They are simply preparing for harvest by planting the seeds. If you look at it that way, you will never question the intensity of your leaders again. What kind of harvest are they preparing for and what kind of harvest are you preparing for in comparison? The fullness of your pantry (and subsequently your belly) depends on the size of your harvest.

If you are not out there marketing and networking your business, you are not prepared to receive business.

Do you work like you want to eat?

Before you can experience success, you must prepare for it. You've got the desire, the vision, and the passion to succeed - now you actually have to build the bridge between you and your dreams. You need a winning team to get to your next stage, but you will never get a winning team without first preparing your mind and body. Get the knowledge and the discipline, and you will get the support and momentum you need.

Prepare to move forward...

Chapter

6

Element 5:
Courage

It takes a brave soul to leave everything that is familiar and pursue the unknown, knowing that the future depends upon the success of the journey. That may sound harsh, but it is exactly what the new entrepreneur (or the entrepreneur who isn't where he wants to be) has to do in order to make it. If you're ever going to see the Promised Land, you're going to have to leave Egypt and go through the wilderness. How long you stay there depends on how fast and well you learn, but if you don't muster up the courage to cross the Jordan River, you'll never make it out. When you have mastered the first two stages of success, you will find yourself needing some courage; this is where you plunge into the deep end, usually not knowing what at all to expect.

How fast and well you learn, will determine the success of your journey.

The third stage, awkward adolescence, is when you find out what you're really made of. You have been driven, you are prepared, but now it's time to sink or swim, and it can be a little scary. You have a team of people who you have convinced of your competence, some training you, some following you, and now if you don't produce, you can actually adversely affect them. Plus, you may lose respect, and more importantly, you won't make money. You have got to put everything you know into practice out there in the big pond with the big fish, no excuses.

Put everything you've learned into practice and perform... no excuses!

Can you handle the pressure?

You can handle the pressure and actually use it to make you more productive if you can do three

things: you must know who you are and what you want, you must separate yourself from those who will hinder you, and you have to focus.

You can handle pressure by knowing who you are and what you want, separating yourself from those that hinder you, and by focusing.

If you are a young woman and I walked up to you and called you a man, what would you do? Would you start doubting yourself and begin to question your gender? Or would you question my intelligence and move on with your life? I should not be able to challenge your gender; in the same way I should not be able to challenge your ability to become financially free. You should have the same response to me if I tell you that owning a successful business is out of reach for you.

Don't allow anyone to challenge your abilities.

All of the elements that you have acquired until this point should give you the basis for your unwavering belief. If you have the desire, vision, passion, and preparation, you can and should have the courage to stand on it when you are faced with opposition. When deals fall through, when hot leads turn into dead ends, when people express their doubts, your courage has to kick in. You have to know that you know that you know that you can do this and that you will do this. You want success too badly and you have worked too hard to let your dreams die now.

Remember, success is natural. Think about it: if you have the first four elements, shouldn't this fifth one naturally arise? The only thing that would prevent you from having the courage you need at

this point is unnatural, negative thinking. The most common source of negative thinking: other people.

Negative thinking is the only thing that can prevent you from having the courage to do anything.

If you don't get anything else from this book, please understand that you absolutely, positively must separate yourself from those who will hinder you. Regardless of whether it is your best friend, your brother, or even your mother, if the people in your circle are doubters, nay-sayers, or critics, you have to distance yourself from them. You may not understand how or why, but if this business is as important to you as you say it is, building it will take up so much of your time that you simply won't be able to afford to give one moment up to negative people. They are time wasters and dream stealers.

You must absolutely, positively separate yourself from those who will hinder you

Are you connected to the wrong crowd?

As you build your team, you may become comrades with one or two 'businesspeople' who are more talk than business. You might be spending too much time listening to someone who's wisdom in other areas is sound, but who doesn't understand what you are doing and is skeptical of your ability to succeed in your endeavors. Some people who don't have the courage that you do are just miserable and are looking for company. Whatever the case, they are planting bad seeds in

your mind, and all that will come up are weeds of doubt which will ultimately lead to failure.

Your words and actions are seeds; plant them on good ground and don't let anyone else plant their bad seeds within you.

Don't let anyone plant bad seeds within you

If you are properly focused, you will realize that these people are bringing you down and that you just don't have the time. Learn from a story about the kind of focus I speak of:

There was once a man who had just found his path to God. He was so excited about knowing God that he wanted to be as close to God as possible. The man went down to the beach to speak with God. As he waded in the surf he began to shout out to God, "I seek you, I want to be closer to you. I desire to be as you would like me to be. Please God; show me how to be close to you." As he waded in the surf about knee deep, he felt a strong, firm hand on his back. The hand pushed him down into the surf and his head underwater.

The young man struggled to be free as his face was pushed into the sand under the water. He struggled as his lungs began to burst for lack of air. He pushed up hard against the strong hand, but had no effect. Finally, when he thought all was lost and that he would drown, the hand released him. As the young man gasped for air, he crawled to the shore. He lay on his back, coughing, wondering what had just happened to him. Suddenly, there was a voice from heaven that said, "When you seek me like you sought

that breath of air, you will be close to me."

When you seek success with all of your heart and soul, you will be on the right path. That young man did not think about how he looked in the surf, suffering. He did not care whether his mother thought he should breathe or not. That young man was focused on one thing; he had a goal of reaching the air and was focusing narrow-mindedly on his goal.

He had focus; where is yours?

Chapter

7

Element 6:
Perseverance

"On you mark, get set, GO!" I'm sure that you felt that way at the starting line, and if you are already at this stage of development, the fourth, sprouting stage, you are plum tuckered out. You have surely invested heavily in your business, both monetarily and with your time, and you may be exhausted. Well, if you are doing this thing the right way, you should be. However, this is the point in which your endurance comes into play. You may have started off sprinting, but it is time for the cross-country run, and only those who can endure make it to the finish line. This is where you really dig deep to find your sense of perseverance.

Endurance is an essential element of success.

This is also the time in which some will accuse you of being fanatical. Those who have never been where you are going will probably begin to preach to you on something I call, "the doctrine of failure". Yes, I know that it's harsh, but it's true. These non-believers, although usually well-intentioned, just don't know enough about building a business to comment, yet they always do. What do they say, you ask? They tell you that instead of being so single-minded in your business ventures, 'you need to find balance'.

Balance is the doctrine of failure.

Balance - the doctrine of failure. You may have been taught this doctrine, and are now shaking your head or reading with caution at this point. While I sympathize with you, I have to disagree, and furthermore, those successful business owners that you strive to be like disagree as well. This

doctrine of failure sounds right at first, if you are following your feelings. However, if you follow logic and facts, you can soon determine that something is wrong with using balance as a roadmap to success.

You do not really want balance; you want victory. Would you complete a great job at work and then balance it with a mistake? Would you prepare a great meal and balance it with garbage on the table? Then why on earth would we seek balance in our business? We want purpose, preparation, execution, and excellence. Start looking at your performance as a race towards dominance, not balance.

You don't want balance, you want victory!

The sprouting stage of development is a unique one; your business will grow in leaps and bounds, but you will be persevering, keeping your endurance up so that you can stay the course. Your business will experience growth spurts because of your consistency. You can't balance that consistency with complacency now. This is no time to take a vacation; you are almost where you need to be, and you must allow nature to take its course. There will be time to sit back and relax soon enough; however, right now you want to press ahead with even more conviction and more focus.

Keep your endurance up and stay the course!

Think about the leaders in your company or industry. How do they act? Do they seem fanatical to you? Think about those you know who are still

struggling to get their businesses off the ground. What do they have in common? Do you see what I mean about following the logic and the facts? It brings you to the realization that balance doesn't create business moguls; perseverance does.

Balance doesn't create success, perseverance does.

So how do you find the inspiration and strength to persevere with so much pressure coming at you from all sides? You do what the rich do.

You don't have a problem with that, do you? While your desire may not be to be filthy rich, I'm sure that you can agree that doing at least some of what they do would help to make you more wealthy, right? What if you did everything that they did? You could possibly become rich without even trying that hard...

It never ceases to amaze me how people in today's America rally together to villainize the rich. In times past, rich Americans like J.D. Rockefeller and Alvah C. Roebuck were inspirations for those who dreamed the American dream. Now, we are taught that the rich are somehow evil because they know how to turn a profit. If we began to study the rich instead of criticizing so much, we just might learn how to become more successful in business ourselves.

Study the rich and learn how to be successful in business.

You're never going to get to the top as long as you resent those who are there. If you make it to

the top, it will be because you became more like them, not less. So learn the three most basic lessons about the habits of the rich. Do the same thing; you will see immediate results. Commit to those changes, and you will find yourself becoming more productive and wealthier by the minute.

You'll never get to the top as long as you resent those who are there.

Rich people control their feelings. Feelings do not control them. The thoughts of a poor person are centered on how he feels. His feelings are his primary source of motivation. "I really do not feel like working today," becomes no work for the day. Relying on feelings keeps poor people poor.

Successful people control their feelings, feelings do not control them.

Rich people control their reasoning. The middle and working-class American looks at work as a means and reason for feeding his family. He goes into debt to cover and feed his family. It seems reasonable for the middle-class person to work towards "retirement", not towards "freedom." It seems logical, and therefore his logic will guarantee that he will not rise above his comfort level. In addition, his children will not either.

Successful people control their reasoning.

Rich people operate on faith. Faith is a verb...not a noun. It is something you are doing based upon your beliefs supported by confidence. Rich people defy the laws of reason. Their motivation is goal oriented. They will achieve their goals in spite of the history. It does not matter how the goal makes them or others "feel", or whether it is a "reasonable" goal or not.

Successful people operate on faith.

This kind of thinking will keep you focused, and that focus will help you to persevere. As your business buds and blooms, your consistency in this stage will establish the foundation that you have worked so hard to create.

Chapter

8

Element 7:
Integrity

The last and final element that emerges to polish the diamond in the rough is integrity. Although you should already possess integrity as an individual, you won't continue to grow and flourish in your last stage of development, managing success, without it. This is when you begin to be recognized as a foremost expert, able to help others climb to where you are, becoming a force to be reckoned with. People will look to you for guidance and mentoring, which will present opportunities for you to either help or cheat them.

You won't continue to grow and flourish without integrity.

Which will you choose?

How many "guru" market books, instructional videos, and seminars prove to be relatively useless?

How much money have you already invested in your business education, only to find that most of the material available on the market today is ineffective in helping one to be truly successful? While there is no golden egg, some businesspeople who have found success are more forthcoming about what it really takes to succeed than others. Many business moguls feel threatened by young entrepreneurs, so they try to keep all of their "secrets" of success to themselves. However, you and I know better; you gain more by giving more. It is not only Godly to do so; it makes good business sense to do everything with integrity.

You gain more by giving more.

Here's why:

When you reach a mature level of success, you garner the trust of those who know you. You have proven that you have what it takes to make it. If you nurture that trust by being honest in your dealings and your advice, your opportunities to benefit financially from your good reputation will exponentially increase. Opportunities to add additional streams of income, either in arenas related to your current business or new business ventures, are made available to you when successful people know that they can trust your reputation. If your integrity is just as solid as your track record of success, you will increase your exposure, your connections, and your profit.

Solid integrity will increase your exposure, connections and profit.

Your good name and reputation are a cash cow; are you going to milk it?

Your integrity also nourishes your existing business. Being honest with your customers at all times, even when it costs you something, makes for long lasting success. With a reputation of superior integrity, you not only gain customers; you gain customer loyalty. Customer loyalty is the cheapest form of marketing there is. It is also the most vital. A loyal customer will brag on you to others. So will a follower or mentee who can honestly say that your influence and advice have changed their lives. Your good name is the best way to both make and save money in business - that means more wealth for you!

Your integrity nourishes your existing business.

So why don't more business owners run their businesses this way? Because most people buy into the notion that we live in a dog-eat-dog world. You might be thinking the same thing yourself. The truth is, however, that such a notion was invented by people who simply needed a way to justify their unscrupulous behavior. When people who appear to be successful tell you that big business is dog-eat-dog, it plants seeds within you that will prevent you from truly blooming after you sprout. You lose respect for the time and money of others, thinking only of your own. Customer service and employee value give way to misleading marketing and substandard products and/or services. You might be thinking, 'Well, that is the way of the world.' That's not true; it's not the way of the world for those who have lasting power.

It's not a dog-eat-dog world, have lasting power, stick to your integrity.

How do you know that, Mason?

It's easy; such beliefs go against nature.

Throughout this book, you have been learning about how success is a natural process. This is the final lesson: it couldn't possibly be true that the business world is dog-eat-dog because it contradicts the truth that you reap what you sow.

You reap what you sow!

Do I need to say that again?

You reap what you sow, period. If you sow dishonesty and ill will that is exactly what you will reap. Your journey through the process of progress should prove that to you. If you ever make it to

this stage of success, it is because you spent the time and energy doing things the right way, staying focused and productive. You don't get to this level playing games or trying to get over. Why? Because nature won't allow you to.

Nature proves that you must sow integrity to reap lasting power.

You must sow integrity to reap lasting power.

Business owners with integrity thrive in any economy. Think about it; despite news reports of rising and falling economic climates, there are some businesses that always whether the storm. Some companies continue to make profits no matter what is going on in the world around them. That happens when customers know what to expect from you and then receive what they expect every time. No tricks, no games; just what you pay for. In business, that is integrity. Businesses that employ such simple tactics always enjoy success. That is why you have to have all of the previous elements of success working for you at this stage; if you keep practicing what nature has taught you, running such an honest business will be natural for you. And so will the increased opportunities that come as a result...

Business owners with integrity thrive in any economy.

chapter

9

A New Season

This is change time! Throughout this book you have learned about the mindset and tools necessary for success in business. Now you have to put what you have learned into action. We are here to make a change in our lives. If you were where you wanted to be, you would not be where you are right now.

It's time to put what you've learned into action. Commit to change!

So commit to changing how you do things. It's not enough to read this book like it is a list of suggestions that you may or may not put into practice. You have to be committed to change, and you have to start right now.

Hunter-Farmer-Orchard Owner

The following story of evolution and change should help you to understand the evolution of an entrepreneur:

The hunter had to wake up every morning and think about getting food to his mouth. He walked the hunting ground in search of prey most of the day. His energy and thoughts were centered around the finding, killing, and preparing of prey. His family had to travel with him and carry everything they possessed.

The hunter could not obtain too many possessions because it would slow him down. He could not spend time teaching his son home building skills because he would need hunting skills to live. There was no community of hunters, only hunting parties, so community skills were never learned. Cooperating was rare because everyone was a competitor and losers died.

Hunters did not survive by developing better hunting techniques or better tools. They did not

survive by finding better hunting grounds. The hunter survived by looking at his circumstances and realizing that he had to change or perish. The hunter survived by becoming the farmer.

He had to leave where he was and develop an entirely new approach to eating. He had to abandon the lessons of his father and grandfather and branch out in a new direction. The hunter had to domesticate the animals he had hunted, and learn how to clear the land and plant the food. The hunter had never been a farmer. No one told him he could be a farmer. He did not have a mentor, he had a need.

It was a hard first step to success, but it was well worth it. The new farmer had more time to train his children, so schools were started. The former hunters and their families could now concentrate on developing individual skills like cooking, building homes, and making tools. Each individual had to leave the lessons of their hunter fathers and concentrate on gaining new skills for community life.

They had a sense of urgency to get the crops planted on time because seasons demanded certain things be accomplished within a particular period of time. If the planting was late, the harvest would be small. If the harvest was late, the crops would be overripe. The new farmer had to maintain his crop and prepare for the new crop simultaneously. He worked just as hard in the winter preparing his barn because he expected a crop in the summer and had to plant in the spring.

The farmers' children had time to contemplate their society. They were able to spend time looking at their circumstances and study them. They realized that if Dad got hurt during the spring and could not get the crops planted they could starve during the winter. They had to develop a better way to survive. Farming was better than hunting, but it still depended upon clearing the land, plowing the fields, planting the seeds, pulling the weeds, watering the crops, and harvesting on time. And then, after you pull up and destroy all of your crops during harvest, you had to do the same next year and every year after. If you missed one step, because of death in the family or injury, you would lose the entire year of food. The land still owned you like a job. You had to work it or not eat. There was little retirement planning or vacation enjoyment. It was a job, all day, everyday.

So what could they do? How could they move the society further along the path of progress? What could they develop in order to escape the burden of working the land?

Someone noticed that they could do the same initial work of a farmer, clearing the land, pulling up the stumps, digging up the earth, and planting seeds, but if they planted fruit trees or a vineyard, something else happened. After a few years of looking after their crop, the crop looked after them. They no longer had to replant every year or even pull the weeds up. Doing the work the right way first, resulted in food for the next year. Not only did it provide food for the next year, but for generations to come. The orchard farmer left an inheritance for his children's children and for generations after.

When the hunter spent time with his children while hunting, he could only teach hunting skills. The farmer spent most of his time teaching farming with a little left over to teach his children how to build a home or road. However, the orchard owner could spend hours under the shade of his trees, teaching his children about managing their money and future. The same amount of work went into developing all three systems, but only one would feed generations. You must decide if you are a hunter, a farmer, or an orchard owner.

Think about your business experience so far; you probably can relate to the hunter and the farmer. Your business endeavors may even resemble a hunting ground or a traditional farm. However, you are most likely to be successful running your business like a vineyard or an orchard.

 It s time to plant your orchard.

What business are you in? No matter what is, there is an orchard there, just waiting to be planted.

The secret is not in the type of business you go into, but your approach to business in your respective field. Look around you, literally. Take a good look at everything in the room that you are sitting in right now. Someone has gotten rich off of every product in your home, from pencils to chairs to the paint or wallpaper on the walls. Do you see what I mean? You don't have to find the latest craze or trend in order to find success; you just have to plant your orchard.

As one who is brave enough to venture out into business, you are truly a diamond in the rough. You now have the tools you need to be refined. Do the work, do it right the first time...

And shine!

To your continued success,

Mason Weaver